WASHINGTON, D.C.
PUZZLE BOOK

Washington, D.C., serves as a testament to American history. From Pennsylvania Avenue to the Potomac River, democracy lives and breathes in our national city, built especially by and for the government. Today, thousands of men and women work in various government offices throughout the District of Columbia, while millions of people from around the world visit its monuments, memorials, and other historical sites each year.

ARCHITECT OF THE CAPITOL

Known throughout the world as an icon of American democracy, our unique seat of government is filled with historic and cultural sites, and this book features several of them, along with fun facts and interesting trivia. Learn more about the monuments to some of our greatest presidents – George Washington, Thomas Jefferson, Abraham Lincoln, Franklin Roosevelt, and about the memorials honoring millions of brave Americans who gave their lives for our country.

Discover how Egyptian, Roman, and Greek architecture influenced many of the structures in the District, and how the specific number of columns, flags, and stars were chosen. Learn about the lives of United States presidents, which one was the first to bring a Christmas tree into the White House, which one didn't speak English at home, and more. Explore the events that started war, preserved the union, and brought together a nation. Read about the places where great Americans lived, fought, and died. Come discover the history of the United States, meet our Founding Fathers, and visit the nation's capital!

PUZZLE ANSWERS ON BACK PAGES

© GRAB A PENCIL PRESS 2017   ISBN: 978-0-9844156-0-1

10 9 8 7 6 5 4 3 2 1

Building a National City — The History of Washington, D.C.

ACROSS

2. Before Washington, D.C., became the nation's capital, Congress convened in this city, where George Washington was also inaugurated in 1789

4. The District was built along the _____ River, which was called, at different times and by different people, Espiritu Santo, Elizabeth, St. Gregory, and Co-hon-ho-roo-ta

5. City planner Pierre L'Enfant's plans called for _____ intersections, revolving around major national sites, such as the Capitol and President's House

8. Built with private funds, the "Brick Capitol" was erected for Congress to hold its sessions until the Capitol was rebuilt after the War of 1812. The United States _____ Court building now sits on that site

9. In 1783, while in Philadelphia, the _____ Congress was confronted by angry unpaid soldiers, prompting the delegates' departure and the necessity for a permanent place to conduct national business

11. Washington, D.C., became the seat of the _____ government six months after George Washington died

12. L'Enfant was instructed by commissioners to use a simple way of naming streets based on letters and _____

13. Virginia became part of the site of the national city after its representatives agreed to vote in support of Alexander _____ "Assumption Bill," by which individual states' debts would be assumed by the federal government

14. During the late 18th century, the increased debate over whether the national city should be in the North or the South led to the original planning of _____ Federal Towns — one on the

Potomac River and one on the Delaware River

15. L'Enfant refused $2,500 and a lot near the _____ House after being fired. He died, in poverty, in 1825

DOWN

1. Though the accuracy of this claim has been debated, it has been said that Benjamin Banneker, a free _____ man and surveyor, memorized and reproduced L'Enfant's plans after his departure, thus allowing construction to continue

3. Called "The Oven," the temporary chamber of the House of _____ was built on the foundation of the Capitol's South Wing

6. Originally, there was some confusion over what to call the national seat. Pierre L'Enfant referred to it as Capital City, Thomas Jefferson called it Federal Town, and George _____ combined the names and called it Federal City

7. During the War of 1812, _____ soldiers marched on Washington and burned nearly all of the public buildings, including the Capitol and the President's House

10. L'Enfant demolished the new manor house of the region's largest _____ because it obstructed a planned vista. This led to the city designer's dismissal

U.S. Capitol

ACROSS

1. The _____ of Congress was once located in the Capitol building, but moved to its own building in 1897

3. The Minton _____ floors feature patterns such as the Greek key and basket weave

4. After crossing this river and marching through the District of Columbia, George Washington laid the cornerstone for the Capitol building on September 18, 1793

6. The _____ is a large circular room located under the dome

8. The Capitol building serves as the home of the United States _____, which is composed of the House of Representatives and the Senate

10. The House of Representatives is housed in this wing

11. The Capitol was built in the neo- _____ style

12. In 1814, _____ troops set fire to the Capitol and the White House during the War of 1812

13. The Capitol _____ Center opened in 2008 after several years of planning and construction. The center offers visitors access to government events, exhibitions, tours, and special events

16. The Statue of _____ adorns the top of the Capitol dome

18. A _____ was held to choose the best design for the Capitol. Dr. William Thornton won

19. Several architects, including Stephen Hallet, George Hadfield, James Hoban (who was the architect of the _____ House), Benjamin Henry Latrobe, and Charles Bulfinch, all contributed to the Capitol's design

20. The Senate is housed in this wing

To learn more, visit www.visitthecapitol.gov

DOWN

1. E Pluribus Unum is a
_____ phrase that means
"Out of many, one"; it is inscribed
under the Capitol dome's statue

2. The National Statuary Hall
Collection features 100 statues,
two from each _____,
honoring historically significant
individuals

5. 17-foot-high, 20,000-pound
bronze doors featuring the life of
explorer Christopher
_____ stand at the main
entrance

7. A painting depicting the signing
of the _____ can be found
in the Capitol

9. Until 1935, the _____
Court, the highest court in the
land, was housed in the Capitol

11. Artist Constantino Brumidi
created the massive fresco
"Apotheosis of George
Washington," dedicated to our
first president; the 13 maidens
in the painting represent the 13
original _____

14. Concerts and fireworks
mark the _____ of July
celebrations at the Capitol

15. In 1793, there were only
15 states, and therefore this
many senators, in the Union. As
more states joined the Union, the
number of congressmen grew,
and the Capitol building needed
to be expanded

17. Congressional _____
Medals are awarded in the Rotunda

Lincoln Memorial

IN THIS TEMPLE
AS IN THE HEARTS OF THE PEOPLE
FOR WHOM HE SAVED THE UNION
THE MEMORY OF ABRAHAM LINCOLN
IS ENSHRINED FOREVER

DAVID BJORGEN

ACROSS

3. In a mural, the Angel of Truth is seen releasing _____ from bondage

9. This proclamation freed the slaves in the Confederate states

10. Above Lincoln's head are the words "In this temple, as in the hearts of the people for whom he saved the Union, the memory of Abraham Lincoln is enshrined _____ "

12. The cornerstone was laid in 1915 on February 12, Lincoln's _____

13. Architect who designed the memorial, Henry _____

16. The Lincoln Memorial, which is modeled after Greek temples, features _____ columns

17. The building is made of limestone and this

To learn more, visit www.nps.gov/linc/index.htm

DOWN

1. The Lincoln Memorial sits at one end of the National _____

2. The Lincoln Memorial was on the back of this coin from 1959 to 2008

3. Type of artwork depicting a sitting Lincoln in the middle of the memorial

4. The two speeches carved in the memorial's walls are his second inaugural address and the _____ Address

5. There are 36 columns in the memorial symbolizing the 36 _____ in the Union at the time of Lincoln's death

6. Lincoln was the _____ president of the United States

7. Name of Lincoln's only surviving son who was present at the memorial dedication in 1922

8. William Howard _____, chief justice and former president, led the dedication ceremonies

11. Civil rights activist _____ Luther King Jr. gave his "I Have a Dream" speech here

14. Lincoln was president during the _____ War. Though the North and South were divided, he tried to preserve the Union

15. A long Reflecting _____ stretches between the Washington Monument and the Lincoln Memorial

Library of Congress — Crack the Code

The Library of Congress is the oldest and largest library in the United States. It was created in 1800 after President John Adams signed a bill to establish a library to be used only by Congress. It was originally located In the Capitol Building. Today, the Library is accessible to all.

The first Library of Congress was burned during the War of 1812. Thomas Jefferson offered to sell his private collection of 6,487 books to Congress to create a new library. His books were the foundation of the new Library of Congress, which soon outgrew its room and needed its own building. Using the Paris Opera House as a model, the Thomas Jefferson Building opened in 1897. Quotes by the former president can be found on the walls of the Library, along with quotes from dozens of other statesmen, philosophers, and writers.

The collection has grown to hold more than 144 million items! It adds 10,000 items to its collection every day and has books in 470 languages. The smallest book found here is one-twenty fifth of an inch by one-twenty fifth of an inch large. It is so tiny that the pages have to be turned by a needle.

There are so many things to see and do at the Library. From reading books to visiting exhibits to enjoying free concerts, the Library is full of discovery!

Thomas Jefferson

To learn more, visit www.loc.gov

Look at the crack the code activity below. The symbols and letters spell a quote by Thomas Jefferson. Use the key to replace each symbol with its corresponding letter and crack the code!

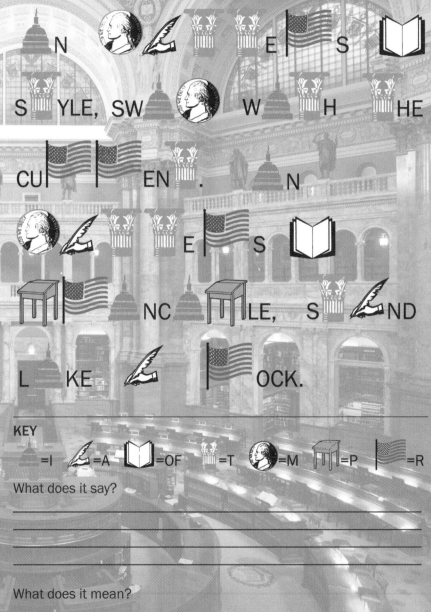

N 🪙 🪶 🏛 🏛 E 🚩 S 📖

S 🏛 YLE, SW 🪙 W 🏛 H 🏛 HE

CU 🚩 🚩 EN 🏛 . N

🪙 🪶 🏛 E 🚩 S 📖

🪑 🚩 NC 🪑 LE, S 🏛 🪶 ND

L 🏛 KE 🪶 🚩 OCK.

KEY

🏛 =I 🪶 =A 📖 =OF 🏛 =T 🪙 =M 🪑 =P 🚩 =R

What does it say?

_____

_____

_____

What does it mean?

_____

_____

_____

The National Archives

ACROSS

2. This inert gas fills an aluminum and titanium encasement that holds the Declaration of Independence

4. The building was designed by prominent architect John Russell Pope, who also designed the Thomas _____ Memorial

9. Before the CIA, the OSS (Office of Strategic Services) was the nation's first centralized _____ agency. The OSS carried out some of its operations in the National Archives building

10. The Declaration of Independence, Constitution, and Bill of Rights were all written on this material

12. President Franklin D. _____ signed legislation creating the National Archives in 1934

13. The doors on the National Archives building are the largest in the world made of this material

15. Before they were transferred to the National Archives, the Declaration of Independence and the Constitution were in the holdings of the Library of _____ from 1921 to 1952

17. Barry Faulkner created _____ that were installed on the walls of the National Archives rotunda in 1936. These depict the presentation of the Constitution and the Declaration of Independence

18. After the Japanese bombed Pearl Harbor, the Constitution

was moved to Fort _____ for safekeeping

DOWN

1. The documents of Japan's surrender at the end of _____ are found in the Archives

3. The pediments at the Archives' Pennsylvania Avenue entrance depict the arts of war and _____

5. The Archives holds the _____ Proclamation, which freed slaves in the Southern states during the Civil War

6. The Declaration of Independence, Constitution, and Bill of Rights are collectively known as the Charters of _____

7. The National Archives is not in just one building in Washington, D.C., but in dozens of facilities across the _____

8. _____ work to preserve important records and share them with the public. They have a deep knowledge of history and

spend many years studying and researching

11. President Herbert _____ laid the cornerstone for the National Archives building on February 20, 1933

14. The National Archives holds billions of records, from the Declaration of Independence to the canceled check from the purchase of _____, which became our 49th state

16. After learning that President Reagan had been shot, Vice President George H.W. _____ began writing remarks on a piece of paper, which is now displayed in the Archives' Public Vaults

Thomas Jefferson Memorial

ACROSS

3. Jefferson chose to have only "Author of the Declaration of American Independence, of the Statute of _____ for Religious Freedom, and Father of the University of Virginia" written on his tombstone

5. The memorial's _____ was modeled after the Pantheon and the Rotunda at Jefferson's University of Virginia

8. The National _____ _____ Festival is held here each spring

9. Jefferson, the third president of the United States, is known as one of the nation's _____ Fathers

13. The 19-foot-tall, 5-ton statue of Jefferson that stands in the center of the memorial looks toward the _____ House

15. Jefferson died on July 4, 1826, 50 years after the adoption of the Declaration of _____

16. Jefferson declared that "Almighty God hath created the mind _____" and that "no man shall be compelled to frequent or support any religious worship or ministry or shall otherwise suffer on account of his religious opinions or belief"

17. The memorial was dedicated on April 13, 1943, the 200th anniversary of Jefferson's _____

To learn more, visit
www.nps.gov/nr/travel/presidents/thomas_jefferson_memorial.html

DOWN

1. Jefferson served as minister to this European country

2. The memorial is adjacent to the Tidal Basin in West _____ Park

4. During World War II, metal was being rationed, so the statue was originally made of _____. It was later replaced by the bronze statue

6. Jefferson was a philosopher and statesman during the Age of _____

7. The memorial was designed by John Russell Pope, who also designed the National _____, which houses the Declaration of Independence

10. According to one memorial inscription, Jefferson swore against every form of "_____ over the mind of man"

11. Franklin D. _____ , who was president during the construction of the memorial, laid the cornerstone in 1939

12. Several of the memorial's inscriptions were taken from _____ that Jefferson wrote to others

14. A sculpture depicts the five members of the Declaration of Independence drafting committee (including Jefferson) submitting their report to _____

World War II Memorial

KRISTEN HALL, RICHMOND, VA

ACROSS

3. "_____ was here," a popular saying during the war, is inscribed on the memorial

5. Number of millions of Americans who served during World War II

6. Memorial pavilions represent two theaters of WWII, the Atlantic and the _____

8. The WWII Memorial is between the Washington Monument and this other memorial

13. The site was dedicated in 1995 on _____ Day, a day of remembrance to honor all those who have served in our military

14. U.S. Senator Bob _____, a WWII veteran, chaired the WWII Memorial Campaign. Actor Tom Hanks was also involved in the campaign

16. Members from all branches of the armed forces gave a musical _____ to the veterans at the memorial dedication

18. The Smithsonian Institution organized a four-day _____ for World War II veterans, so they could reconnect with fellow service members and visit the new memorial

19. The 405,000 American deaths in World War II are symbolized by a wall with more than 4,000 gold _____

DOWN

1. President who ordered the bombings of Hiroshima and Nagasaki, which led to the end of the war with Japan

2. The name of the wall in the memorial lined with gold stars

4. More Americans died in WWII

To learn more, visit www.wwiimemorial.com

than in any other war except the
_____ War

7. Most of the money raised to build the memorial was not from the government; it came from private contributions, including donations from individual American _____

9. Women at home joined the war effort, working in factories and building tanks and military planes, ships, and equipment. Collectively, these hard-working females were nicknamed Rosie the _____

10. WWII saw the integration of women into the _____ forces when Congress created the WAAC (Women's Army Auxiliary Corps)

11. The United States entered WWII after Japan attacked _____ _____ on December 7, 1941

12. Number of pillars that arch around the memorial, one for each state, district, and territory of the United States

13. On May 8, 1945, Nazi Germany officially surrendered to the Allied forces; this day of victory is known as _____

15. President Bill _____ signed the law authorizing the establishment of the WWII Memorial

17. President George W. _____ was in office when the memorial was dedicated in 2004

Washington Monument

ACROSS

1. Construction slowed because of political uncertainty, and stopped during the _____ War

3. George Washington was called the "_____ of His Country"

4. Dedicated in 1885 on February 21, the day before Washington's _____

6. Chester A. _____ was president at the time of the monument's completion

8. The monument sits in an area that stretches from the Lincoln Memorial to the Capitol, known as the _____ Mall

10. In 1996, the monument underwent _____, which included extensive sealing, cleaning, and repairing

11. Number of years it took to complete the monument and open it to the public

13. The cornerstone of the monument was laid in 1848, on _____ Day

16. Washington was a member of the _____, a fraternal organization spanning the globe. Members of this organization were present at the dedication

UNITED STATES AIR FORCE

To learn more, visit www.nps.gov/nr/travel/wash/dc72.htm

17. Many individuals, states, and countries donated memorial _____, which were inserted in the interior walls

18. Architect who won the contest to design and build the monument, Robert _____

19. The Washington Monument is surrounded by 50 _____

DOWN

2. Though some wanted Washington to be buried at the monument, he was interred at his Virginia plantation, Mount _____

3. Was the world's tallest structure until the Eiffel Tower was built in this country

5. Because of the decades-long delay in building, the bottom part of the monument is a different _____ from the rest

7. Due to lack of funds, the Washington National Monument Society was temporarily under the control of the Know-_____, a political party

9. In 1833, prominent Americans John Marshall and James _____ founded the Washington National Monument Society, dedicated to creating a memorial to the first president

12. The Washington Monument is modeled after a type of Egyptian structure known as an _____

14. The monument is managed by the National _____ Service

15. To reach the top, visitors originally had to climb 897 _____. Now, they use an elevator

Arlington National Cemetery

U.S. ARMY/KATHLEEN T. RHEM

ACROSS

1. A memorial honors the First U.S. Volunteer Cavalry, also known as the _____ Riders, led by Teddy Roosevelt

5. The Memorial Amphitheater's cornerstone, which was laid on October 15, 1915, by Woodrow Wilson, contains 15 items, including a copy of the Constitution and this religious book

6. Arlington National Cemetery is administered by the Department of the _____

9. A memorial was dedicated to the _____ Guard after it lost two cutters, and the lives of all those onboard, during World War I

10. For those who are _____ instead of buried, a columbarium houses their remains

11. Flags in the cemetery are flown at _____ every weekday that funerals are held

12. On average, the cemetery conducts 28 _____ per day

14. This kind of flame marks the grave of John F. Kennedy, the youngest man elected president, who was assassinated in 1963

15. George Washington Parke Custis, the adopted grandson of George Washington, was the original owner of the land on which Arlington Cemetery now

To learn more, visit www.arlingtoncemetery.org

sits. Custis' daughter, Mary Anna Randolph Custis, was married to Confederate General Robert E. _____

16. Former slaves were resettled in _____ Village, now the southeast section of Arlington National Cemetery

DOWN

2. The Tomb of the _____ serves as a memorial to honor all service men and women who died anonymously

3. More than _____ hundred thousand people are buried at the cemetery

4. This is sometimes laid on a grave in remembrance during formal ceremonies and observances

7. Thurgood _____, who is buried at Arlington, was the first black man to be appointed as a Supreme Court justice

8. The parkway known as _____ Drive extends across the Potomac River and leads visitors to Arlington National Cemetery

9. The land was converted to a cemetery during this war

10. A memorial dedicated to the crew of this space shuttle, which exploded after liftoff in 1986, was erected at the cemetery

13. William Howard _____ was the first president to be buried at Arlington; he also served as chief justice of the United States Supreme Court

58,000 Names —
Vietnam Veterans Memorial

ACROSS

7. Frederick Hart, describing the three soldiers in his statue, said: "There is about them the physical contact and sense of unity that bespeaks the bonds of love and sacrifice that is the nature of men at war. And yet they are each _____. "

DEPT. OF DEFENSE/SGT. SARA WOOD

8. Jan Scruggs, a Vietnam _____, led the campaign to create a memorial

10. The Memorial Wall was made from polished _____, chosen for its quality of reflection

11. The last names on the Memorial Wall are those of 18 Marines who were killed during a _____ operation, weeks after the official end of the war

14. An education center is located _____ so as not to take away from the memorial

15. The symbol of a diamond beside some names represents those who have _____

16. The names are listed in _____ order of their captured, missing, or killed dates

18. The Memorial Wall was _____ in 1982

19. The Memorial Wall was _____ by Yale student Maya Lin, who wanted to "convey the sense of overwhelming numbers while unifying those individuals into a whole."

DOWN

1. The $8.4 million required to create the memorial was raised entirely by _____ donations

2. The symbol of a cross next to some names denotes those who were _____ in action

3. The Vietnam _____ Memorial focuses on the important contributions of nurses during the Vietnam War. Their role had been largely overlooked until this sculpture — marking the first time female patriotism was honored in a memorial

4. The inscribed dedication on the West Wall reads, "Our nation honors the courage, sacrifice, and _____ to duty and

To learn more, visit www.vvmf.org

country of its Vietnam veterans"

5. In 1982, during the memorial's construction, a _____ Heart was placed in the concrete. This began the tradition of leaving offerings at the Wall. Over the years, everything from flags and flowers, dog tags and uniforms, medals and pictures, teddy bears, and even a motorcycle have been placed at the Wall

6. The Wall is 246 feet _____ and comprises 70 panels

9. The first names on the _____ Wall are those of Charles Ovnand and Dale Buis, who were killed by communist guerillas

12. The Three _____ Statue depicts a Hispanic soldier, a black soldier, and a white soldier, all looking toward the Memorial Wall. This represents unity among the military

13. Those who are unable to visit Washington, D.C., can still see a version of the Memorial Wall. "The Wall That _____" features a half-size replica that travels from city to city, giving many the opportunity to experience the Wall

16. The names of the nurses of the Vietnam Women's Memorial are Hope, Faith, and _____

17. The fall of _____ was on April 30, 1975, and marked the official end of the divisive Vietnam War

White House Scramble

For hundreds of years, presidents of the United States have lived in the White House. Though George Washington was our country's first president, he was not the first to live in the White House. Construction began in 1792 and did not end until after Washington's term of office. John Adams, the second president of the United States, was the first to reside in the White House. Since then, countless press conferences, meetings, and speeches have happened here.

The White House has more than 130 rooms, 55,000 square feet, a swimming pool, a putting green, a bowling alley, and a movie theatre. Thomas Jefferson said that the White House was "big enough for two emperors, a pope, and the grand lama."

Read the quotes about the White House below. Each one was made by a president of the United States. Try to unscramble the names to find out which president said what.

I never forget that I live in a house owned by all the American people and that I have been given their trust.

V E O S R O T L E = _____

Sometimes I wake at night in the White House and rub my eyes and wonder if it is not all a dream.

D C L L E E V A N = _____

Since I came to the White House, I got two hearing aids, a colon operation, skin cancer, and I was shot. The thing is I've never felt better in my life.

G A N E R A = _____

The White House: I don't know whether it's the finest public housing in America or the crown jewel of the prison system.

N I C L N T O = _____

Throughout his presidency, Abraham Lincoln spent the warmer months at what is now called President Lincoln's Cottage. A National Historic Landmark, the cottage is located in northwest Washington, D.C., and served as a much-needed place of rest for the president and his family. They spent one-quarter of his presidency here.

Try to unscramble the words below to learn the original name of President Lincoln's Cottage, which was used by retired and disabled veterans.

O S S D R E L I   O H E M = _____ _____

To learn more, visit www.whitehouse.gov

Landmark Supreme Court Cases

The Supreme Court is the highest court in the United States. Nine justices, who are appointed by the president and must be approved by the Senate, sit on the Court. The justices' job is to make sure the country's laws follow the Constitution. They uphold, overturn, and make decisions based on the Constitution. Many of the most important cases are decided by the Supreme Court. Below are a few of the cases that the Supreme Court has heard. Use the word bank to fill in the blanks and learn how their decisions changed the country.

BROWN v BOARD OF EDUCATION

The Supreme Court reversed the 1896 decision of *Plessy v* _____, which stated that segregation was allowed in schools under the "_____ but equal" clause. The Supreme Court then decided that schools could not be equal unless they were desegregated.

UNITED STATES v NIXON

It was revealed that _____ Nixon had tapes concerning the _____ scandal and refused to turn them over. He believed he had executive privilege and didn't have to follow the law because he was the president. The Supreme Court ruled against him and he was impeached.

MARBURY v MADISON

This case helped establish _____ review in the United States. It helped to define the limits of powers in each branch of government – _____, executive, and judicial.

MIRANDA v ARIZONA

Ernesto Miranda was arrested and questioned for hours before confessing to a crime. However, he was never advised of his rights to remain _____ or receive _____. Because of this, his confession was thrown out and now law personnel must inform suspects of their rights, known as their "Miranda rights."

WORD BANK

counsel	Ferguson	judicial	legislative
Richard	separate	silent	Watergate

To learn more, visit www.supremecourt.gov

Franklin Delano Roosevelt Memorial

ACROSS

4. There are four outdoor rooms in the memorial, each one representing a four-year _____ of office

8. _____ Roosevelt is the only first lady to be honored with her own statue at a presidential memorial

10. FDR said, "The test of our progress is not whether we add more to the abundance of those who have much; it is whether we provide enough for those who have too _____."

11. The FDR Memorial is located along Washington, D.C.'s famous _____ Tree Walk

12. At one of the statues, _____, Roosevelt's dog, sits next to the president

15. The memorial is arranged so that visitors may walk through four expansive rooms that detail Roosevelt's terms in office, his actions, and his words in _____ order

17. One theme of the memorial is Roosevelt's New _____, which launched several programs aimed at helping struggling Americans. These programs included Social Security, workers' compensation, welfare, and unemployment insurance

DOWN

1. Several sculptures in the memorial were created by world-renowned artist George _____

2. The "Breadline" sculpture attempts to capture the plight of the Great _____, with hungry men lining up for some much-needed food

3. A statue of Roosevelt sits at the entrance to the memorial. The president is sitting in a _____, which was concealed from the public during his years as a political leader

5. In Room 3, there is a large _____, with the flow of water hindered by large granite blocks, symbolizing the effects of World War II

6. "The only limit to our realization of tomorrow will be our doubts of _____. Let us move forward with strong and active faith." These words, written by Roosevelt but never delivered because of his death, are etched into the memorial

7. One quote by Roosevelt reads, "I have seen war. I have seen war on land and sea. I have seen blood running from the wounded. I have seen the dead in the mud. I have seen cities destroyed. I have seen children starving. I have seen the agony of mothers and wives. I _____ war."

9. A commission was set up in 1955 to construct a memorial in honor of President Roosevelt, but the design was not chosen until 1978, and the memorial was not completed until 1997, when it was dedicated by President Bill _____

13. The memorial was designed to be wheelchair- _____. Also, Braille is available in raised relief for the visually impaired

14. FDR gave weekly radio addresses known as "_____ chats." During one of them, he said, "We defend and we build a way of life, not for America alone, but for all mankind."

16. The "Four Freedoms" etched in the memorial are the Freedom of Speech, Freedom of Worship, Freedom from Want, and Freedom from _____

Freedom Isn't Free —
Korean War Veterans Memorial

COL. JOHN CHAPMAN, USA (RETIRED), RICHMOND, VA

ACROSS

3. The 38th Parallel is the _____ line between North and South Korea

5. Harry S. _____ was president at the beginning of the Korean War

6. The Pool of _____ honors the dead, wounded, imprisoned, and missing. Their statistics are engraved in stone nearby

8. Inscribed on a plaque at the memorial: "Our nation honors her sons and daughters who answered the call to defend a country they never knew and a _____ they never met"

9. U.N. forces helped liberate _____, the capital of South Korea

11. 15,000 _____ of the war from the National Archives were used to create the images on the wall

13. 19 _____ were sculpted by Frank Gaylord. Each is over 7 feet tall, adding a sense of heroism to the soldiers

14. The United States had a great number of _____, with more than 150,000 dead or wounded

15. Thinking the war was almost over, U.N. forces were taken by surprise when 300,000 _____ troops, who had been hiding in North Korea, attacked them

16. The national _____ of South Korea, the rose of Sharon hibiscus, is planted at the memorial

17. 22 members of the United _____ took part in the

To learn more, visit www.nab.usace.army.mil/projects/WashingtonDC/korean.html

Korean War. The names of these countries are engraved on the curbstone

18. The statues are made of stainless _____ and sculpted to look lifelike, with wind-blown ponchos and emotional facial expressions

19. The statues depict members from all _____ of the military, as can be observed in the different uniforms

DOWN

1. The Korean War lasted more than _____ years

2. The _____ Roll lists all those killed or missing in action, as well as prisoners of war

4. The DMZ is short for the _____ Zone

7. The Korean War marked the beginning of America's campaigns against _____

10. The _____ Wall was designed by Louis Nelson. It is 164 feet long and is made up of 41 panels

11. The wall creates the image of 38 statues, symbolic of the 38th _____ and the 38 months of war

12. United States President Bill Clinton and the President of _____ _____, Kim Young Sam, dedicated the memorial on July 27, 1995

Public Service

President John F. Kennedy stated, "Ask not what your country can do for you; ask what you can do for your country."

There are many ways citizens can serve their country. They can get involved in politics by becoming educated and well-informed about issues facing the world. They can exercise their right to vote. They can also actively participate in public service programs that help those in need. There are many programs in the United States that people can join, all with the goal of helping others.

Look at the word bank below and try to find all the words related to public service.

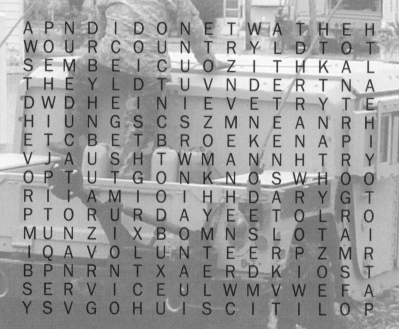

```
A P N D I D O N E T W A T H E H
W O U R C O U N T R Y L D T O T
S E M B E I C U O Z I T H K A L
T H E Y L D T U V N D E R T N A
D W D H E I N I E V E T R Y T E
H I U N G S C S Z M N E A N R H
E T C B E T B R O E K E N A P I
V J A U S H T W M A N N H T R Y
O P T U T G O N K N O S W H O O
R I I A M I O I H H D A R Y G T
P T O R U R D A Y E E T O L R O
M U N Z I X B O M N S L O T A I
I Q A V O L U N T E E R P Z M R
B P N R N T X A E R D K I O S T
S E R V I C E U L W M V W E F A
Y S V G O H U I S C I T I L O P
```

WORD BANK

CITIZENS	COUNTRY	EDUCATION	ENVIRONMENT
HEALTH	HELP	IMPROVE	PATRIOT
POLITICS	PROGRAMS	PUBLIC	RIGHTS
SERVICE	SHARE	VOLUNTEER	VOTE

PUZZLE ANSWERS

Building a National City —
The History of Washington, D.C.

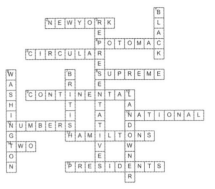

U.S. Capitol

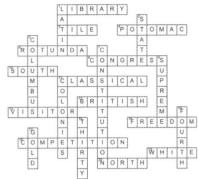

Lincoln Memorial

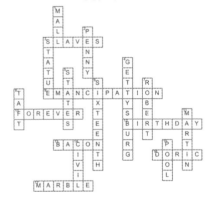

Library of Congress
Crack the Code

In matters of style, swim with the current. In matters of principle, stand like a rock.

The National Archives

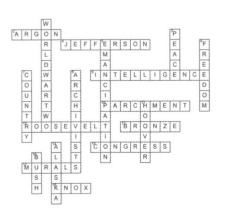

Thomas Jefferson Memorial

World War II Memorial

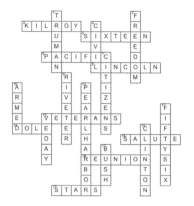

Washington Monument

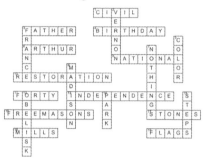

Arlington National Cemetery

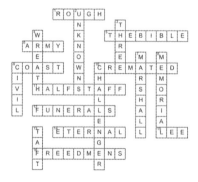

White House Scramble

Roosevelt
Cleveland
Reagan
Clinton
Soldiers Home

58,000 Names —
Vietnam Veterans Memorial

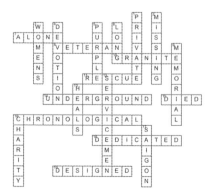

Supreme Court Fill in the Blank

Brown v Board of Education
Ferguson
separate

United States v Nixon
Richard
Watergate

Marbury v Madison
judicial
legislative

Miranda v Arizona
silent
counsel

Franklin Delano Roosevelt
Memorial

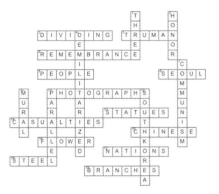

Freedom Isn't Free —
Korean War Veterans Memorial

Public Service Word Search

```
A P N D I D O N E T W A T H E H
W O U R C O U N T R Y L D T O T
S E M B E I C U O Z I T H K A L
T H E Y L D T U V N D E R T N A
D W D H E I N I E V E T R Y T E
H I U N G S C S Z M N E A N R H
E T C B E T B R O E K E N A P I
V J A U S H T W M A N N H T R Y
O P T U T G O N K N O S W H O O
R I I A M I O I H H D A R Y G T
P T O R U R D A Y E E T O L R O
M U N Z I X B O M N S L O T A I
I Q A V O L U N T E E R P Z M R
B P N R N T X A E R D K I O S T
S E R V I C E U L W M V V W E F A
Y S V G O H U I S C I T I L O P
```

TOPICS
GRAB A PENCIL PRESS

Abraham Lincoln
American Flag
American Revolution
Architecture
Art History
Benjamin Franklin
Civil War History
Ellis Island and the Statue of Liberty
First Ladies
Flight
George Washington
John Fitzgerald Kennedy

National Parks
Natural History
New York City
Presidents of the United States
Secret Writing
Texas History
Thanksgiving
Vietnam War
Washington, D.C.
World War II
World War II European Theater
World War II Pacific Theater

Yellowstone National Park

COMING SOON
Black History Puzzle Book
Gold Rush Puzzle Book
Korean War Puzzle Book
Library of Congress Puzzle Book
Women's History Puzzle Book
World War I Puzzle Book

USA GRAB A PENCIL PRESS

an imprint of Applewood Books
Carlisle, Massachusetts 01741
www.grabapencilpress.com

To order, call: 800-277-5312